D1480888

The 1910s

Stephen Feinstein

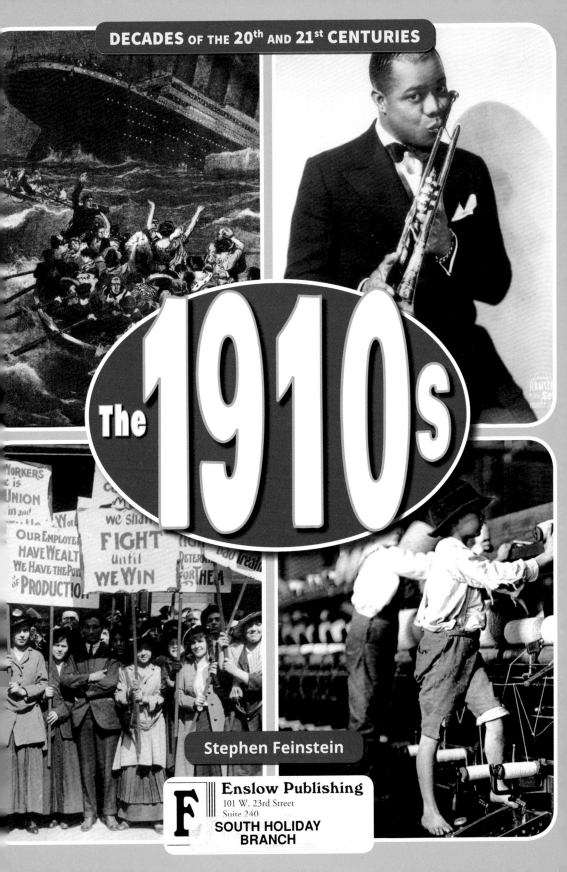

The 1910s

Stephen Feinstein

Enslow Publishing
101 W. 23rd Street
Suite 240

Published in 2016 by Enslow Publishing, LLC.
101 W. 23rd Street, Suite 240, New York, NY 10011

Library of Congress Cataloging-in-Publication Data

Feinstein, Stephen.
The 1910s / Stephen Feinstein.
    pages cm. —(Decades of the 20th and 21st centuries)
Summary: "Discusses the decade 1910-1919 in the United States in terms of culture, art, science, and politics"—Provided by publisher.
Audience: Grade 9 to 12.
ISBN 978-0-7660-6922-0
1. United States—Civilization—1865-1918—Juvenile literature. 2. United States—Politics and government—1913-1921—Juvenile literature. 3. United States—Politics and government—1909-1913—Juvenile literature. 4. Nineteen tens—Juvenile literature. I. Title.
E169.1.F3539 2015
973.91'2—dc23
                            2015010943

Printed in the United States of America

To Our Readers: We have done our best to make sure all Web sites in this book were active and appropriate when we went to press. However, the author and the publisher have no control over and assume no liability for the material available on those Web sites or on any Web sites they may link to. Any comments or suggestions can be sent by e-mail to customerservice@enslow.com.

Contents

The "unsinkable" Titanic hit an iceberg, sank, and killed more than 1,500.

Introduction

Progress does not mean the end of problems—that was the lesson of the 1910s. During the first decade of the twentieth century, Americans had made great gains. They saw many advances in science and technology, and they lived in the richest nation in the world. This progress would continue during the 1910s. However, there would also be many terrible disasters during this decade that would slow society's zeal for rapid growth. By the end of the decade, many people longed for a simpler time.

Some of the disasters during the 1910s showed that science and technology did not hold all of the answers. One example was the sinking of the supposedly unsinkable *Titanic* in April 1912. Later in the decade, a deadly flu epidemic spread across the globe. All the advances of modern medicine could not stop a tiny virus from causing an illness that killed millions of people.

Science and technology were not always applied in peaceful or benevolent ways, either. New factories created modern weapons that made it easier to kill. In August 1914, these terrifying weapons were unleashed and used by millions of soldiers in World War I. This war was the worst tragedy of the 1910s. It killed ten million people.

At first, Americans felt the war was strictly a matter involving European countries. But when German submarine attacks claimed American victims, the president sent American soldiers into the war to fight on the side of Great Britain, France, and other countries known as the Allies. Their enemies were Germany, Austria-Hungary, and their allies, which were called the Central Powers.

As American soldiers fought overseas, the Bolshevik Revolution occurred in Russia. Vladimir Lenin became the ruler of the world's first communist nation. Many Americans began to fear that a communist revolution could happen in America. In 1919, a Red Scare (communists were often called Reds) swept the nation. Also that year, the worst race riot of the decade occurred in Chicago.

America helped the Allies win the war, but US president Woodrow Wilson could not convince them to agree to a fair peace treaty. To punish the Central Powers for starting the war, the Allies enforced crippling fines and took land from Germany and its allies to build up their own empires. This caused deep bitterness in the people of the defeated nations. Without realizing it, the treaty's authors had sown the seeds for another world war.

American soldiers returned from the battlefield to find that important changes were taking place at home. Throughout the 1910s, women tried to earn the right to vote. Americans approved the Seventeenth Amendment to the US Constitution, which allowed senators to be elected by the people. This was considered a major progressive accomplishment. Many immigrants arrived from other countries and hoped to become US citizens. A young film industry took root in Hollywood, California. By the end of 1919, Americans did not want to hear any more about wars or bad news from overseas. After a decade of disasters, Americans were ready to have some fun.

Pop Culture, Lifestyles, and Fashion

By 1910, America had become the richest nation in the world. As such, it acted as a magnet and drew millions of people from around the world seeking a better life for their families.

Immigrants Arrive in Record Numbers

As if in response to the invitation engraved on the Statue of Liberty—"Give me your tired, your poor, your huddled masses yearning to breathe free"—millions of immigrants arrived at Ellis Island in New York Harbor to begin a new life in America. Many were fleeing religious, racial, or political persecution. Most hoped to escape a life of dire poverty. For the millions willing to endure the hardships of immigration, America was indeed a promised land. In 1910, the massive wave of immigration that had begun in 1890 was at its height. That year, more than one million immigrants, primarily Jews, Slavs, and Italians from eastern and southern Europe, entered the United States. Most settled in the large cities of the Northeast and Midwest, where factories needed workers. Immigrants from Asia, most of them Chinese, arrived on the West Coast at Angel Island in San Francisco Bay.

By the middle of the decade, many native-born Americans were becoming alarmed at the huge influx of newcomers. Recent immigrants

Immigrants flocked to America in search of opportunity.

spoke foreign languages and had different religions, customs, cultural values, and political views. Assimilation into American society was a slow and difficult process for many immigrants. Anti-immigrant feelings began to grow.

Responding to this pressure, Americanization programs were established in schools around the country. Adult immigrants were taught English, as well as courses in American cooking, house-keeping, and childcare. The government also passed the Immigration Act of 1917. This law imposed a literacy test for immigrants. It also prohibited Asian laborers from entering the country, except for those from nations that had special trade agreements with the United States. Immigration did, in fact, drop sharply during the years of World War I because of wartime restrictions and the difficulties of traveling during a war, and the new law caused a further decrease. Even so, by 1920 more than eighteen million immigrants had come to America during the thirty-year period beginning in 1890.

The Great Black Migration

Adding to the explosive population growth in the cities were millions of Americans from rural areas. They, too, sought job opportunities. Among this group were more than 330,000 African Americans from the rural South. An editorial in the *Chicago Defender*, a leading African-American newspaper of the time, encouraged blacks to leave the racial violence, discrimination, and poverty of the South and move to cities in the North. The fall-off in immigration during the war years was causing labor shortages in the North, and factories were eager to hire black workers to fill jobs. Once the United States entered World War I in 1917, even more jobs became available for African Americans. Many blacks went north to take advantage of this opportunity. This mass movement of blacks to the North became known as the Great Migration.

Race Riots

Rural Southern blacks moved to cities in the South, as well as the North. Unfortunately, this migration led to racial clashes in many cities. Long the victims of racial discrimination and violence in the rural South, African Americans now faced the hostility and resentment of urban whites who did not welcome them. The National Urban League, founded in 1910, worked to help rural African Americans adapt to city life.

The National Association for the Advancement of Colored People (NAACP), formed in 1909, waged legal battles to win voting rights for blacks. It also organized protest demonstrations throughout the decade. In 1917, ten thousand African Americans marched in New York City to protest lynchings.

African-American activism provoked a violent reaction from white racists. The white supremacist organization known as the Ku Klux Klan (KKK), which had been dormant for many years, sprang back to life with renewed vigor on December 4, 1915, when it was granted a charter by the state of Georgia. Back in business, the KKK promoted hatred of blacks, as well as Jews and Catholics.

In 1917, seventeen whites were killed in a riot in Houston that started after police beat an African-American soldier. Nineteen black soldiers were later executed. The same year, forty-eight people died in a race riot in East Saint Louis. In 1919, twenty-five major race riots occurred. The worst of these took place in Chicago that summer. It began after a young African-American swimmer was killed when he and three friends tried to use a "white" beach on Lake Michigan. Thirty-eight people were killed, and more than five hundred were injured in the week of violence that followed.

The National Guard was called to Chicago in response to race riots.

The Triangle Shirtwaist factory fire resulted in strict labor laws.

A Deadly Fire Results in New Labor Laws

Many young immigrant women in America found jobs in garment industry sweatshops. The hours were long, the pay was low, and the working conditions were terrible. In 1910, the average American worker earned less than fifteen dollars for working a fifty-four- to sixty-hour week. Those who worked in sweatshops such as the Triangle Shirtwaist Company in New York City, who were mainly young Jewish and Italian women, earned even less than that. Nevertheless, they were glad to have a job. At Triangle, they sewed tailored blouses on a piecework basis and were paid by how many pieces they produced.

The owners of the Triangle Shirtwaist Company, Max Blanck and Isaac Harris, were known as the Shirtwaist Kings. They kept the stairway exit doors of their factory locked to prevent theft. On March 25, 1911, a fire broke out. The employees were trapped inside. The only way to avoid burning to death was to jump out the windows. Forty-six young women jumped to their deaths from the ninth floor. Another one hundred died inside the building. The Shirtwaist Kings were indicted for manslaughter, but they beat the charge with the help of their lawyer, Max Stever. The tragedy resulted in new labor laws in New York, including a fifty-four-hour workweek for women and children. Fifty-seven laws were passed concerning workplace safety, as well as laws covering workers' compensation.

Child Labor

Employers who hired women usually paid them less than male employees, which is why women were hired in the first place. Unions, such as the International Ladies' Garment Workers' Union (ILGWU), fought for a better deal for women. However, other unions did not try to help women workers. Male union members often saw women as competitors for the best jobs.

Employers in many industries liked to hire children because they could pay them even less than they paid women. During the 1910s, more than six hundred thousand children worked on farms. Thousands of others worked in mines, mills, and factories. The work was often dangerous and exhausting. Since its formation in 1904, the National Child Labor Committee had been working to end child labor. Finally, in the 1910s there was some progress.

In 1912, the US Children's Bureau was established. It was directed by Julia Lathrop, the first woman to head a federal agency. In 1916, there were still almost two million children working in the United States. That year, Congress passed the Keating-Owen Child Labor Act. It prohibited interstate shipment of goods made by children. It also prohibited children under the age of sixteen from working more than eight hours a day, from working at night, and from working in dangerous places, such as mines. In addition, the law established fourteen as the minimum age for all other types of work.

Wobblies and the Labor Movement

In the 1910s, skilled workers, such as carpenters and bricklayers, organized into trade unions affiliated with the American Federation of Labor (AFL). The AFL, under the leadership of Samuel Gompers, was not interested in representing America's unskilled workers, who made up around 95 percent of the workforce. Unskilled workers were often victims of the worst abuses of the profit-driven capitalist system. Desperately in need of representation to win higher pay and better working conditions, these individuals joined unions such as the Industrial Workers of the World (IWW) and the United Mine Workers of America (UMW). While the AFL was politically conservative, IWW organizers, referred to as Wobblies, often held radical political views. At times, they even said that the overthrow of the capitalist system was the only way for workers to get a fair deal.

Young children worked long hours in factories and on farms.

Wobblies gather in New York City's Union Square in 1914.

Wobblies organized many strikes during the 1910s. In January 1912, thousands of workers at the textile mills in Lawrence, Massachusetts, began a strike that lasted two months. The mills had cut the workers' salaries, which had barely been above starvation level to begin with. Before the strike was over, a young Italian striker named Annie LoPezzi was shot dead by a soldier. IWW organizers, among them Elizabeth Gurley Flynn and William "Big Bill" Haywood, were finally able to restore the workers' pay. IWW membership in Lawrence increased to ten thousand mill workers.

In September 1913, in Ludlow, Colorado, nine thousand miners who were members of the UMW went on strike. They were employees of mines owned by John D. Rockefeller. At the time, the miners were paid $1.68 a day. Their salary was paid by scrip instead of cash. Scrip was not ordinary money. It could be used only in Rockefeller stores and as rent for Rockefeller shacks. The strike lasted seven months. Before it was over, many strikers died.

On October 17, several miners were killed in gun battles with armed guards. On April 20, 1914, three hundred guards, some firing machine guns, attacked a miner's camp near Ludlow. When they burned the tents, two women and eleven children who had been hiding in an underground bunker suffocated. Above ground, five miners were killed by gunfire, and more than one hundred were wounded. Among the dead was strike leader Louis Tikas. He had been captured, beaten, and shot in the back. During the following days, forty more people were killed before federal troops sent by President Woodrow Wilson restored order. Sadly, the strikers' demands were not met.

In 1915, six striking workers were killed by guards at the Standard Oil refinery in Bayonne, New Jersey. That same year, Joe Hill, who had been arrested in January 1914 for killing a Salt Lake City grocer, was executed by a firing squad. He had been convicted on flimsy evidence. The forty-three-year-old Wobbly songwriter became a legend as people around the world rallied to his defense.

Within a few years, the IWW itself would come to the end of its road. During World War I, many people came to believe that the IWW was antiwar and unpatriotic. IWW membership plummeted. IWW leaders were arrested or deported. By late 1918, the IWW was no longer a force in the labor movement. But the labor scene would heat up again once the war was over.

Radical Reds

In 1919, there were more than twenty-six hundred strikes in the United States. Four million workers—one out of every five—walked off the job. Major strikes occurred in industries from steel to coal mining to railroads. Seattle was the scene of a general strike, and in Boston, thousands of police officers went on strike. Adding to the turmoil was a series of bombings around the country. People began to fear that striking immigrant workers were Reds, or communists, plotting the overthrow of the government.

On June 2, 1919, the Washington, D.C., home of A. Mitchell Palmer, the recently appointed Attorney General, was bombed. In response, Palmer, aided by J. Edgar Hoover, planned a massive crackdown on anyone who seemed radical. From November 1919 until February 1920, the Palmer-Hoover raids rounded up thousands of alleged communists, socialists, and anarchists. Most of these people were immigrants. Hundreds were deported. The Red Scare had a chilling effect on union activity. The labor movement did not fully recover until the 1930s.

Marching for a Cause

Throughout the 1910s, Americans by the thousands took to the streets for a variety of causes. African Americans marched for an end to discrimination. Pacifists marched to oppose America's participation in World War I. Prohibitionists—members of the Women's Christian

Workers strike for improved labor conditions in 1919.

Jeanette Rankin

Casting the deciding vote for the Nineteenth Amendment in the House of Representatives was Jeannette Rankin, who, on April 2, 1917, took her seat as the first woman elected to serve in Congress.

Jeannette Rankin was born in Montana in 1880. As a young woman, she attended college. Later, she fought for women's suffrage in Montana and the state of Washington. Rankin wanted to prove that a woman could also hold political office. She successfully ran for a seat representing Montana in the US House of Representatives in 1916. In Congress, Rankin helped write new laws aimed at improving health care for children and mothers. She also opposed US involvement in World War I and helped to establish the American Civil Liberties Union. Still active today, this group works to defend and preserve the individual rights and liberties guaranteed to all American citizens by the Constitution and national laws.

Temperance Union (WCTU) and the Anti-Saloon League—marched to win support for a ban on the manufacture and sale of alcoholic beverages. Their efforts were rewarded when, in 1919, a law was ratified—the Eighteenth Amendment to the Constitution.

Also successful were the suffragists. Led by organizations such as the National Woman's Party (NWP) and the National American Woman Suffrage Association (NAWSA), suffragists marched to demand the right to vote for women. In 1919, Congress passed the Nineteenth Amendment. After it was ratified in 1920, women were granted the right to vote.

Margaret Sanger

Public health nurse Margaret Sanger practiced nursing on the Lower East Side of New York City. While working with poverty-stricken immigrants, she came to believe that one cause of poverty is families that are too large to be adequately supported. After seeing women die from illegal abortions, Sanger saw the need for a national program of birth control. In 1914, she founded the National Birth Control League and began publishing a magazine called *The Woman Rebel*. This led to her first arrest because at that time, it was illegal to distribute birth control information or devices in the United States. In 1916, Sanger opened the first birth control clinic in the United States in Brooklyn, New York. Again she was arrested and was sent to prison. But Sanger would continue to fight for women's rights for the rest of her life.

The *Titanic* Tragedy Shocks the World

Millions of people during the 1910s journeyed across the high seas. For the vast majority of them, specifically immigrants crowded in cramped quarters, the voyage was not especially enjoyable. The ships were not exactly luxurious. But for the other ocean travelers, such as wealthy families on vacation abroad or captains of industry traveling on business, the ocean crossing was often pleasurable and relaxing. For the wealthy, the great transatlantic ocean liners provided every imaginable luxury. The world soon learned, however, that money could not always shelter a person from tragedy.

The biggest ship of its time, the British ocean liner *Titanic* was believed to be unsinkable. Longer than a city block, this floating hotel had nine decks and could carry more than 3,500 people. Though large, it could move across the water quickly. The *Titanic* set off on its first voyage on April 10, 1912. It left from Southampton, England, en route to New York City. Many famous and wealthy people were aboard, including Colonel John J. Astor, one of America's richest men, and his young bride. The ship featured luxurious cabins and elaborate meals. Lower classes also traveled on the ocean liner, although in decidedly less grand accommodations.

The *Titanic* had completed about two thirds of its maiden voyage when it reached iceberg fields off Newfoundland. Just before midnight on April 14, 1912, the *Titanic* struck an iceberg and began taking on water. At first, the crew did not realize the extent of the damage, but the iceberg had torn long gashes in the side of the ship. The *Titanic* had been built to withstand some damage, but not this much. Water began rushing into the gashes, and the ship was sinking.

The captain gave the order to abandon ship, but the process went slowly. Many guests were still asleep and had to be woken up and led to lifeboats. Even worse, the *Titanic* did not have enough lifeboats. There was only enough room on the lifeboats for about half of the passengers on the ship.

As people plunged into the icy water, the ship sank in less than three hours. Some 1,500 of the ship's 2,340 passengers and crew died. Most quickly froze to death. Some of the victims were millionaires. Others were immigrants hoping for a better life in America. The *Titanic* tragedy led to a number of safety reforms. New laws required

The tragedy of the Titanic is still of interest today.

lifeboat space for all passengers on a ship. The International Ice Patrol was formed to spot dangerous icebergs. New methods were developed for rescues at sea.

Americans Die in *Lusitania* Sinking

A few years later, another ocean liner met a similar fate, but for a different reason. On May 7, 1915, the British ship *Lusitania*, said to be the fastest and largest passenger liner then in service, was en route from New York City to Liverpool, England. It was a sunny afternoon, and the green hills of Ireland were visible on the horizon. Suddenly, without warning, the *Lusitania* was struck by torpedoes from a German submarine. The liner sank within eighteen minutes. Among the 1,198 dead were 128 American citizens. The unfortunate passengers had entered a war zone.

Until the *Lusitania* sinking, America had remained neutral during World War I. President Wilson viewed the conflict as European empires fighting for more power. America's neutrality did not extend to trade, however. US companies were more likely to do business with Britain and France than with Germany and its allies, and as a result were fueling the Allied war effort. German U-boats had orders to sink any ship that might be carrying war supplies to the Allies.

The sinking of the *Lusitania* and killing of civilians outraged many Americans. President Woodrow Wilson warned Germany that further attacks on US citizens would not be tolerated. Wilson still wanted to keep America out of the war. Within two years, however, America would declare war on Germany and attribute it to that country's submarine warfare against American passenger and commercial ships.

Henry Ford's Assembly Line

During the 1910s, the automobile was gaining in popularity every day. Those who could afford a car bought one. Those who could not

Boy Scouts of America

In 1909, a wealthy American named W. D. Boyce was visiting London. While walking through the city, he became lost. A young boy helped him back to his hotel. Boyce offered a tip, but the boy refused. He explained that he was a Boy Scout and had to do a good deed every day. Impressed, Boyce decided to learn more about Scouting.

A British Army General named Robert Baden-Powell had startead the Boy Scout program in Great Britain. The purpose of Scouting was to help young men become productive members of society. In 1908, Baden-Powell wrote a guide for the program called Scouting for Boys.

When Boyce returned to America, he met with several men who had previously begun other youth troops that shared the goal of teaching boys useful social skills. They decided to incorporate these groups into one, the Boy Scouts of America, which was established in 1910.

Scout troops were soon started in many American cities and towns. At first, the program was open to boys between the ages of eleven and sixteen. Outdoor activities, such as camping and hiking, were used to teach boys how to be self-reliant and resourceful. Troop leaders tried to show Scouts how to be good citizens who helped others.

dreamed about someday owning one. In 1910, hundreds of different makes and models were available that ranged in price from a Sears Model L for $370 to a $2,500 Cadillac.

Car manufacturers also had a dream—to sell thousands of automobiles. Henry Ford succeeded in making this dream a reality. He had begun manufacturing his Model T in 1908 with the goal of making a reliable car that was affordable to a huge number of potential buyers. That year, Ford sold more than eighteen thousand Model Ts. Sales of the Model T, or Tin Lizzie, as it was nicknamed, kept doubling over the next few years. But this was not good enough for Ford. He was determined to find ways of cutting the cost of production. This, in turn, would allow him to lower the cost to the consumer and let many more Americans buy a car.

By 1913, Ford and his mechanics had created an assembly line. Instead of having one worker build a complete car at his own work station, the frame of the car would move from one end of the factory to the other as workers each built one portion of it. Along the way, workers would add axles, wheels, and other parts as the car passed by. This dramatically increased the number of cars that could be made and greatly decreased the cost of building them.

Throughout the decade, more and more cars appeared on the roads. Roadside businesses sprang up and catered to automobile travelers. The first drive-in gas station opened for business in 1913. People used their cars to run errands, to go shopping, and to go to church. Going for Sunday drives and family picnics in the country became favorite pastimes. Venturing forth to distant towns and scenic attractions became common ways to spend a vacation. Picture postcards grew very popular with travelers, who were eager to show the folks back home where they had been and what they had seen.

Dancing gained in popularity to the disapproval of many.

Juliette Low and the Girl Scouts

Concern for the welfare of children, as evidenced by the new child labor legislation, was on the minds of many during the 1910s. Among them was Juliette Gordon Low, known affectionately as Daisy. Low dreamed of giving America "something for all the girls." What she had in mind was an organization that would give young girls an outlet for their abilities, similar to the Boy Scouts of America. Low wanted girls to have the opportunity to experience the outdoors and perform voluntary public service-oriented tasks in their own communities.

Daisy Low started her organization in 1912 in Savannah, Georgia, with a group of eighteen girls. Low's Girl Scouts were soon happily hiking and camping. Low's ideas spread quickly, and troops of Girl Scouts formed all over the country. In 1915, a national organization made up of the various Girl Scout troops was incorporated as the Girl Scouts of America.

Animal Dances

Ordinary Americans worked hard in the 1910s, but they also liked to have a good time. And nothing was more fun than dancing, especially to the popular music of the day known as ragtime. Americans danced at parties, night clubs, and restaurants. They took dance lessons and participated in dance contests. New dance steps seemed to appear daily. The tango became widely popular in 1910 but was quickly followed by one fad after another.

Never before had dancing been so popular with so many people. But while the dancers enjoyed themselves, critical voices complained that the new dance steps were shocking or even immoral. Some critics referred to the new dances as animal dances. America's most popular ballroom-dancing couple, Vernon and Irene Castle, helped to appease critics. The Castles described themselves as a "clean-cut" young married couple who made dancing look like fun without being at all suggestive. They conveyed the message that dancing was not only moral, but it was also good exercise.

Women's Fashion

In the spring of 1910, designers in Paris, France, believed they had created the last word in fashion elegance when they introduced the hobble skirt to American women. It was very long, reaching down to the ankles, as had been typical of skirts and gowns for many years. However, this particular item was often tied near the hem by a straight band. Anyone wearing such a garment was literally hobbled, or almost prevented from walking. In reaction to the Parisian hobble skirt, in October 1910, the American Ladies' Tailors Association introduced a suffragette suit. This new style included a skirt that was divided down the middle. Women who wore the suffragette suit could walk freely and take long, bold strides.

Ballroom dancer Irene Castle played an important role in influencing women's fashion in America. She liked dresses with simple, flowing lines that would leave her legs free for dancing, as well as skirts that were slightly shorter than the traditional style. She wore slips and bloomers instead of corsets and petticoats. And when she cut her hair short before undergoing surgery, she appeared later with a pearl necklace around her head, which kept her bobbed locks in place. Because she was so popular, women all across America began to imitate her look.

Irene Castle's bobbed hair and flowing skirts became all the rage.

Entertainment and the Arts

The dance craze that was sweeping the country during the 1910s led, in turn, to a popular song craze. But music was moving in surprising directions, as were all the arts.

Tin Pan Alley and the Musical Revue

Millions of Americans fell in love with the tunes they danced to, and they rushed out to buy sheet music versions of those songs. Thousands of titles were available in the music stores, and singers known as pluggers would perform songs at the request of a customer. The songs were a product of Tin Pan Alley, the sheet music companies in New York City that hired composers to create the songs. Among the biggest hits of the decade were George M. Cohan's songs about the war, such as "Over There" and "Till We Meet Again," George Gershwin's "Swanee," and Irving Berlin's "Alexander's Ragtime Band."

Phonograph record sales took off in a big way once recorded versions of popular hit songs became available. In the previous decade, recorded music usually consisted of classical music and opera. Records now became so popular that sheet music sales were in a steep decline by the end of the decade. The most popular recorded songs were derived from either ragtime or the blues.

George Gershwin (1898–1937) wrote the hit "Swanee" in 1919.

Another musical entertainment of the 1910s, the musical revue, could be found on New York's Broadway and in theaters around the country. These were essentially variety shows. They consisted of songs and elaborate dance numbers draped around a simple plot idea. Victor Herbert, Irving Berlin, and George Gershwin were among those who wrote songs for these shows. The most famous musical revue was the *Ziegfeld Follies*. It featured the beautiful Ziegfeld Girls and entertainers, such as Fanny Brice, Eddie Cantor, Will Rogers, and W. C. Fields. Other variety shows, known as vaudeville and burlesque, also attracted large audiences. Many comedians who would later become famous—including Jack Benny, George Burns, Buster Keaton, Jimmy Durante, and the Marx brothers—got their start in the variety shows of the 1910s.

Jazz Soothes the Nation

A new type of music called jazz became popular in the 1910s. African-American musicians invented jazz in the South, and New Orleans quickly became the genre's epicenter. Early jazz bands used a variety of instruments, such as the trumpet, violin, and clarinet. The new music was lively, and people often danced to it. Jazz musicians often improvised, or added their own personal style to songs. Bandleader Buddy Bolden was one of the first jazz musicians to add his own style to the new form of music. Other early jazz musicians to achieve fame were pianists Jelly Roll Morton and James P. Johnson, saxophonist Sidney Bechet, cornetist Joe "King" Oliver, and trumpeter Louis Armstrong.

After the 1910s, many jazz musicians moved from New Orleans to Chicago as part of the Great Migration, a larger movement of African Americans from the South to the North. In Chicago, the jazz movement continued to grow until eventually jazz became a national form of music enjoyed by millions.

Louis Armstrong

Louis Armstrong was a brilliant trumpet player. He helped make early jazz music popular. Armstrong was born in New Orleans in 1901. By the time he was eighteen years old, he was thrilling audiences with his musical ability.

Armstrong was a master of improvisation. He created exciting new sounds with his trumpet. In later years, he also used his powerful voice. Armstrong was among the first to use scat singing. With scat singing, he would insert silly sounds and syllables, such as "razzamatazz-bee-bop" into the song. Sometimes he simply imitated the sound of an instrument.

Louis Armstrong's nickname was Satchmo. It was short for "satchel-mouth," a reference to his large mouth. He remained a premier American performer until his death.

Birth of the Hollywood Star

The movie industry was born during the first decade of the twentieth century. Most film production companies at that time were located in New York City. During the 1910s, the industry shifted to Hollywood because southern California's weather and scenery were better for outdoor filming. Major changes quickly followed. Short one-reel films,

Charlie Chaplin became known for his character the Little Tramp.

typical of the previous decade and the early 1910s, evolved into full-length feature films.

D. W. Griffith, considered America's first great film director, produced the first twelve-reel feature films—*The Birth of a Nation* (1915) and *Intolerance* (1916). Griffith developed new film techniques and made use of them in these films, both of which are considered classics of the silent screen despite their racist messages. *The Birth of a Nation* glorified the Ku Klux Klan and portrayed its members as heroes saving the white race from corrupt, dangerous African Americans.

Other movie directors focused on specific genres of film, including Westerns and comedies. Thomas Ince directed Westerns that starred cowboy heroes, such as Tom Mix and William S. Hart. Mack Sennett made comedies starring the Keystone Kops, Charlie Chaplin, and other comedians who relied on slapstick routines, wild car chases, and pie throwing.

One of the biggest changes in the film industry was the creation of the Hollywood star. During the previous decade, even the most important actors in a film were treated no differently from movie extras today. They were poorly paid, and movie audiences knew next to nothing about them. In the 1910s, however, film studios came to realize that publicity about particular actors would create a following among the public and lead to higher ticket sales. Soon, American moviegoers were flocking to the theaters to see their favorite actors, such as Mary Pickford, Douglas Fairbanks, Lillian Gish, and Gloria Swanson, who quickly became major stars.

Cubists and Dadaists

An art critic at the 1913 Armory Show in New York described artist Marcel Duchamp's painting *Nude Descending a Staircase* as "an explosion in a shingle factory." To the untrained eye, the nude in the semiabstract painting might not be immediately apparent. The

New Authors, New Ideas

Long before television and the Internet, people looked to books for entertainment. During the 1910s, a new wave known as modernism swept the arts. Literature was no exception.

James Joyce was one of the first modernist authors. The Irish author's books did more than simply describe people, places, and things, but they also expressed his characters' views and feelings. It was a unique approach to storytelling that allowed readers to see what the story's characters were thinking. One of Joyce's most famous novels was *A Portrait of the Artist as a Young Man*, published in 1916. A later novel, *Ulysses*, is considered one of the finest books ever written.

Like Joyce, British writer Virginia Woolf (*above*) was a modernist. Woolf's books also explored inner thoughts and feelings, and she particularly liked to show how each person might react differently to the same event. *The Voyage Out*, published in 1915, was her first novel. She wrote many other books afterward, including *Mrs. Dalloway* (1925) and *To the Lighthouse* (1927), as well as her long essay *A Room of One's Own* (1929), that are still studied and read today.

During the 1910s, Nebraska-born author Willa Cather wrote four best-selling novels. Many of her works are about life on the American prairies of the Midwest. *My Ántonia*, published in 1918, is considered her finest work.

painting belonged to a new artistic style known as Cubism. In it, people and objects were fragmented and portrayed at the same time from many different angles.

The Armory Show included works by other European artists, such as Claude Monet, Auguste Renoir, Vincent van Gogh, Georges Seurat, Paul Gaugin, and Henri Matisse. The works of American painters, such as James Whistler, Mary Cassatt, Edward Hopper, and George Bellows, were also featured. The exhibit later traveled to other American cities, including Chicago and Boston. It was eventually seen by thousands of Americans.

In 1917, a group of European artists known as Dadaists exhibited their work in New York. Their goal was to reject all traditional values of art. According to them, anything could be considered art—even a urinal, which was exhibited as *The Fountain*, a sculpture by Marcel Duchamp. The Dadaists, like the Cubists, had found yet another way to outrage the art critics.

Heavyweight champion Jack Johnson's success enraged many racists.

Sports

The war affected all parts of life, including sports. The 1916 Summer Olympics were scheduled to take place in Berlin, Germany, but as the fighting raged on, it became clear that they would not take place. Still, there were plenty of sports taking place on the home front.

Jack Johnson

From 1908 until 1915, the world heavyweight boxing title was held by African American Jack Johnson. Many racist white Americans were outraged that a black fighter had the title. Spurred on by the comments of racist sports writers and fight promoters, white boxing fans yearned for the day when a "Great White Hope" would come along and reclaim the heavyweight boxing title. On July 4, 1910, it seemed as if their prayers were about to be answered. A white boxer, former heavyweight champion James J. Jeffries, stepped into the ring with Johnson in Reno, Nevada. Fifteen rounds later, Jeffries, after taking a punishing beating, received a left hook to the jaw. He went down and stayed down. Johnson was still the champ. White racists went on a wild rampage of violence against blacks. At least eight people were killed.

Jack Dempsey

Boxing was very popular in the 1910s. Born in Colorado, Jack Dempsey was a beloved boxer who would become a star in the next decade. Dempsey's family was poor, and his father moved them around the country in search of work. As a youth, Dempsey earned a living by boxing for money in taverns or small clubs. He then became a professional fighter. He amazed fans with his strength and ability to take punches without being knocked down. In 1918, he won an amazing fifteen bouts and lost just one. A year later, Jack Dempsey captured the world heavyweight championship. He would defend the title many times.

The next championship bout took place in Havana, Cuba, on April 5, 1915. In the twenty-third round, Johnson lost his title to white boxer Jess Willard. Willard, in turn, lost the title to Jack Dempsey on July 4, 1919.

Jim Thorpe, the World's Greatest Athlete

"Not for me," said Swedish athlete H. Weislander, a participant in the 1912 Summer Olympics in Stockholm, Sweden. Weislander was refusing to accept the gold decathlon medal. "I did not win the decathlon. The greatest athlete in the world is Jim Thorpe." Norway's F. R. Bie refused to accept the gold pentathlon medal, as well, saying, "Thorpe won the pentathlon. The medal belongs to him." These two Olympic athletes could not in good conscience accept the medals that had been taken from American Indian Jim Thorpe.

In 1912, Thorpe had become the first Olympic athlete to win both the decathlon and pentathlon. Swedish King Gustav V, upon presenting the medals to Thorpe, said, "Sir, you are the greatest athlete in the world." Thorpe became an American sports hero overnight.

The very next year, the International Olympic Committee (IOC) learned that Thorpe had previously earned money playing semiprofessional baseball from 1909 to 1911. The IOC took the gold medals away from Thorpe. In the eyes of the committee, Thorpe was not an amateur athlete and therefore should not have participated in the Olympics.

Thorpe was bitterly disappointed. He claimed to have been unaware of any violation of the Olympic amateur code. Prevented from competing in amateur sports, Thorpe turned to professional sports. From 1913 to 1920, he enjoyed various stints with several professional baseball and football teams. In 1950, he was named the outstanding male athlete and best football player of the first half of the twentieth century in an Associated Press poll of sports writers. In 1982, the IOC finally gave Thorpe's 1912 gold medals back to his family.

Horse Racing and the Indy 500

Thoroughbred horse racing became an increasingly popular spectator sport in the 1910s. Various racetracks around the country began to hold races, known as stakes races. In these, owners of horses paid an entry fee that became part of the prize for the winner. Previously, the prize money had come from the spectators' admission fee. By far the most exciting year for horse racing fans was 1919. That year, Sir Barton won the Kentucky Derby, the Preakness Stakes, and the Belmont Stakes, which made him the first horse in America to win the Triple Crown.

Not all races involved horses, however. As the automobile began to play an important role in the lives of Americans, it was not long before automobile racing captured the attention of millions. In 1909, a two-and-a-half-mile racetrack called the Brickyard was built near Indianapolis, Indiana. Automobile manufacturers used the track to test new cars they were developing. Races were also held there. On Memorial Day in 1911, the first five-hundred-mile automobile race was held at the Brickyard. The winner was Ray Harroun, who drove a car known as a Marmon Wasp. The race generated so much excitement that the Indy 500, as it came to be called, became an annual tradition.

The Chicago Black Sox

Americans could forget about the war for an afternoon by enjoying baseball. By the 1910s, baseball was the most popular sport in America. The decade 1910–1919 saw the construction of many ballparks that could hold large crowds.

However, a cheating scandal rocked that sport in 1919. Seven players from the Chicago White Sox secretly accepted money to lose the World Series on purpose. The guilty players, along with another player who had refused to take part in the fix but did not tell the authorities beforehand, were banned from the major leagues for life. Disgusted fans referred to the team as the Black Sox.

National and International Politics

The first two decades of the twentieth century, often referred to as the Progressive Era, were a time for reform in politics. Progressive legislation of the 1910s included a federal income tax law (the Sixteenth Amendment to the Constitution), antitrust laws, child labor laws, and the Eighteenth Amendment to the Constitution, which outlawed alcoholic beverages.

Progressive Candidates

In keeping with the spirit of reform, Americans elected reform-minded politicians to lead the nation. In the 1910s, reformers from every part of the political spectrum could be found running for office from conservative Republicans who supported antitrust legislation to socialists, such as Eugene Debs, who believed that the capitalist system was to blame for all of America's problems. According to Debs, true reform would mean dismantling capitalism and replacing it with socialism, where the government runs businesses.

In 1912, Republican president William Howard Taft was running for reelection. Former president Theodore Roosevelt rose to challenge him for the nomination during the Republican primary. Roosevelt was still popular with American voters, as he had earned a reputation as a

Alcohol was poured down drains and into rivers.

trustbuster during his two terms in office a decade earlier. In a speech in Osawatomie, Kansas, in August 1910, he had lashed out against "the sinister control of special interests."

When Roosevelt failed to win the Republican nomination, more than three hundred progressive Republican delegates split from the party. They formed the Progressive party and nominated Roosevelt for president. An energized Roosevelt bellowed to the newspapers, "I'm feeling like a bull moose!" For a time, Roosevelt seemed invincible. On October 14, 1912, in Milwaukee, a would-be assassin shot Roosevelt in the chest as he stood in an open car. He had been on his way to make a speech. Although the bullet had entered his right lung,

Eugene Debs cofounded the Wobblies and ran for president five times. As a Socialist Party leader, Debs strove to drive out capitalism.

Income Tax

In 1913, Congress passed the Sixteenth Amendment to the Constitution, which allowed the US government to collect income taxes, a tax based on the money that people earn from work and other sources. The government created what is called a graduated income tax because the rate of taxation is divided into regular stages or levels. People who earn more money pay more in taxes. People who earn less money pay less.

Prior to 1913, the US government had collected revenue through property taxes and tariffs. A property tax is based on the value of a citizen's possessions, such as land. A tariff is a tax on products that come from other countries. Many Americans were glad to see the change to an income tax. They viewed it as a fair method of paying for government services, especially since the country expected the federal government to do more. Because most people have an income, they share in the burden together.

Some Americans opposed the progressive income tax. They argued that high tax rates were not fair to the wealthy. They also said that taxes would stop rich people from investing in business ventures. The income tax still has its critics today.

Roosevelt insisted on continuing to the hall, where he said, "I will make this speech or die!" Roosevelt made his speech. He did not die, but he did not win the election either. The split among Republicans weakened their party, and the election went to the Democratic candidate, Woodrow Wilson, Governor of New Jersey and a former university professor.

The Mexican Revolution ushered in years of political unrest.

A Civil War in Mexico

The citizens of Mexico, America's neighbor to the south, also believed that their country needed reform. Indeed, many Mexicans were ready to take up arms to bring about change. As a result, Mexico underwent a decade of violent upheaval.

In early 1910, Francisco Madero had sought to become a presidential candidate in Mexico. He was arrested and exiled by Mexican president Porfirio Díaz, who had ruled as a dictator since 1876. Madero wanted to bring democracy to Mexico, along with better working conditions and land for the poor farmers who made up a majority of the population. Calling for revolution, Madero returned to Mexico, organized an army, and, in November 1910, began an insurrection.

Popular leaders won power in different parts of the country— Francisco "Pancho" Villa in the north and Emiliano Zapata in the south —and joined the revolution, each raising an army. The revolutionaries quickly won victories against Díaz's forces. On May 25, 1911, Díaz resigned from office. Madero was elected president the following November.

But Mexico's troubles had just begun. Madero could not control the powerful forces that opposed him. In 1913, General Victoriano Huerta led a coup against the government. Madero was forced to resign the presidency and thrown in prison. A week later, he was executed. Meanwhile, Huerta declared himself dictator of Mexico.

For the next few years, a state of civil war existed. Zapata and Villa allied with Venustiano Carranza, and the three led their armies against Huerta. In 1914, the revolutionaries overthrew Huerta, and in August, Carranza took over the government.

The United States allowed Carranza's troops to cross American territory to attack Pancho Villa from the north. Villa became so enraged at this that he crossed the United States-Mexican border with his troops and attacked the town of Columbus, New Mexico, by burning buildings and killing seventeen Americans. He also attacked a train in Mexico on March 9, 1916, which killed seventeen American mining engineers on board. On March 10, an angry President Woodrow Wilson ordered General John Pershing to capture Villa. More than five thousand United States troops crossed the Rio Grande into Mexico. They returned home empty-handed, as they were unable to find Villa.

Ultimately, more than a million Mexican citizens died during the years of civil war, including revolutionary leaders. In 1919, Carranza's soldiers set a trap and murdered Zapata. The following year, Carranza was assassinated during a coup by his former general, Alvaro Obregón, who became president. He and his successors carried on the revolutionary ideals and tried to improve the government. In 1923, Villa was murdered by political enemies.

The Panama Canal

While Mexico was caught up in the tumult of revolution, history of a different sort was being made farther south. On August 15, 1914, the Panama Canal opened for shipping. The fifty-one-mile-long canal through the jungles and mountains of Panama had taken the United States ten years to build, although work had been done by other nations since 1880. In 1903, a grateful Panama, having just won its independence from Colombia with American help, gave the United States a ten-mile-wide zone across Panama in which to build the canal. With the opening of the canal, ships sailing between the Atlantic and Pacific oceans no longer had to travel all the way around Cape Horn at the southern tip of South America. The Panama Canal, controlled by the United States, would soon become a major avenue of world trade.

The Panama Canal was a breakthrough in shipping.

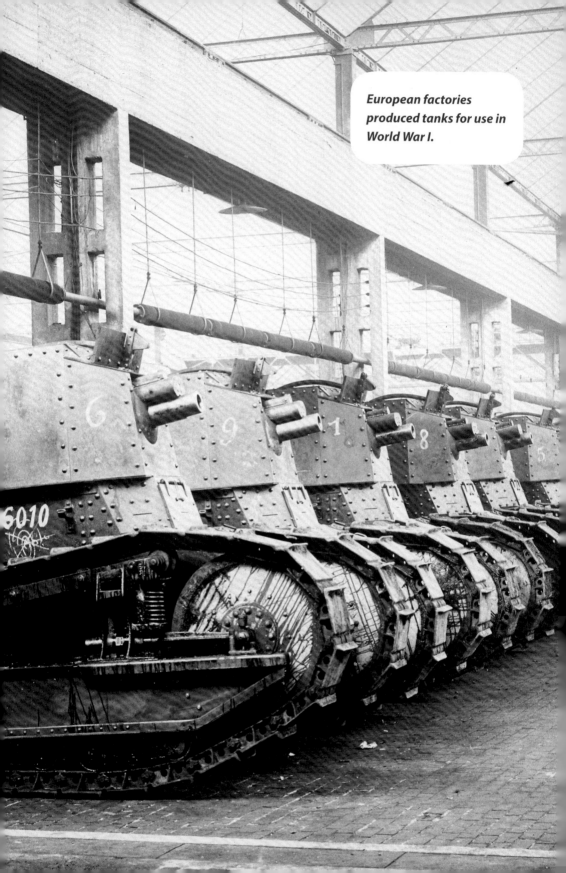

European factories produced tanks for use in World War I.

The Great War Begins

On June 28, 1914, a tragic event occurred in the Bosnian capital of Sarajevo. Archduke Franz Ferdinand, heir to the throne of Austria-Hungary, and his wife, Sophie, were shot to death as they rode in an open car. The assassination, tragic in itself, had serious implications for millions of other people. The assassin was Gavrilo Princip, a Serbian revolutionary. At the time, Bosnia was a province of Austria, while Bosnia's next door neighbor Serbia was independent. Many Bosnians, as well as Serb nationalists, were opposed to Austrian rule. They preferred either an independent Bosnia or a Bosnia under Serbian rule.

Up until this moment, peace had prevailed in much of Europe for several decades. A balance of power had been achieved through a complex system of alliances among nations. The two major alliances were the Triple Entente (Great Britain, France, and Russia) and the Triple Alliance (Germany, Austria-Hungary, and Italy). But the peace created by these alliances was shaky. Nationalistic feelings were growing stronger, and the major powers were involved in a massive arms race. Adding to the tensions were various unresolved conflicts, such as territorial disputes and economic rivalries, that simmered in the background. By 1914, Europe had, in many ways, become a tinderbox.

The assassination of the Archduke was the spark that started the fire. Austria-Hungary blamed Serbia for the assassination. On July 28, Austria-Hungary declared war on Serbia. Two days later, Russia, Serbia's ally, began moving its armies toward its borders with Austria and Germany. On August 1, Germany declared war on Russia, and two days later, on France, Russia's ally. Wasting no time, German troops invaded Belgium on their way to attack France. The next day, August 4, Great Britain declared war on Germany. By the end of August, many thousands of soldiers had already been killed in the fighting, and millions of others were preparing to join the war.

Great Britain, France, and Russia were known as the Allies. Within nine months, they were joined by Italy. Germany and Austria-Hungary, known as the Central Powers, would soon be joined by Turkey and Bulgaria. Fighting spread to parts of the Middle East and even to some parts of Africa. Australia and New Zealand sent troops to help the Allies. In 1914, Japan, declaring war on Germany, took the opportunity to seize German colonies in China and the Pacific.

America Enters World War I

By early 1915, the German Army had become bogged down on the battlefields of France. A stalemate developed. Although casualties continued to climb at a staggering rate, neither side made much progress. The Germans began using poison gas. Before long, both sides were using it.

As the war raged on, Americans were happy that the wide Atlantic separated them from the war-torn European continent. Most Americans did not want to get involved. In fact, Woodrow Wilson was reelected president in 1916 partly because, as his campaign reminded voters, "He kept us out of war."

Meanwhile, combatants in the war used new technology in hopes of gaining an advantage. In addition to poison gas, armored tanks were used for the first time in battle. Improved machine guns saw widespread use. Airplanes were also used in combat for the first time to drop bombs on the enemy and to engage in dogfights with enemy planes. But it was the German use of submarines, or U-boats, that would change the course of history.

Early in 1917, Germany tried to set up a naval blockade around Great Britain while hoping to starve the English into defeat. The Germans announced a policy of unrestricted submarine warfare against all ships entering England's waters. All ships, military or not, would be subject to attack. German submarines began firing torpedoes at every

The War from the Air

Still a new invention during the 1910s, the airplane became an important weapon during World War I. At first, planes were used to spy on enemy ground troops. From the air, a pilot had a good view of the battlefield. He could see where enemy soldiers were hiding. He could also warn his side of an enemy attack.

Soon there were many planes in the air. When a pilot came across an enemy airplane, he fired at it with a pistol or shotgun. After a while, each side began mounting machine guns on their airplanes to shoot each other down. A pilot who shot down five enemy planes was called an ace.

The first air aces were German, French, and British. Germany's Manfred von Richthofen, nicknamed the Red Baron, scored eighty victories before he was shot down in April 1918. America's top ace was Eddie Rickenbacker, a racecar driver. Rickenbacker shot down dozens of enemy aircraft and received the Congressional Medal of Honor for his heroics.

German attacks on US vessels swayed public opinion toward war.

ship unlucky enough to cross their path, including neutral American merchant vessels. Soon, the Germans were sinking an average of six ships a day.

President Wilson was coming to the conclusion that America might not be able to remain neutral much longer. Then in February 1917, Great Britain gave the US government a telegram sent from Arthur Zimmermann, Germany's foreign secretary, to Germany's ambassador in Mexico. The British had intercepted the message and decoded it. It instructed the German ambassador to tell the Mexicans that if they became Germany's ally in the war, Germany would help them retake the lands Mexico had previously lost to the United States—most of the southwestern United States. The message was made public. Coming as it did on top of news of several terrible German submarine attacks, it caused outrage among most Americans. Pressure began to build for war against Germany.

On April 2, 1917, President Wilson declared that "the world must be made safe for democracy" and asked Congress to declare war on Germany. Fifty members of the US House of Representatives opposed entering the war against Germany. Among them was Jeanette Rankin, who had just taken her seat in the House as the first woman to be member of Congress. A pacifist from Montana, Rankin said, "I want to stand by my country. But I cannot vote for war." Despite Rankin's vote, America entered the war on the side of the Allies.

American Indians in the War

Gertrude Bonnin and other young American Indians had founded the Society of American Indians in 1911 and began publishing *American Indian Magazine* in 1916. As many as sixteen thousand Indian men left the reservation and served in the military during World War I. By that time, most Indians were US citizens and were therefore eligible for the military draft. Some Indians opposed the war and the draft.

They felt no love for a country that had mistreated them for so long. But according to Cato Sells, Commissioner of Indian Affairs, at least three-quarters of all Indians in the military had enlisted.

Revolution in Russia

In November 1917, for the second time that year, Russia was shaken by revolution. In March, Tsar Nicholas II had been forced to step down from his throne, which brought an end to a three-hundred-year-old monarchy. Three years of participation in World War I had led to shortages of food and fuel in Russia. The public, now growing war-weary, threatened civil unrest. Millions of starving workers and peasants, who were living in conditions of appalling poverty, resented the wealthy few. In the capital of St. Petersburg, the Tsar's guards refused to fire on a crowd of angry protesters. Instead, many of the soldiers joined the demonstration.

When the Tsar stepped down on March 12, a provisional government was established under the leadership of Alexander Kerensky. But the new government was weak, and talk of revolution remained in the air. People were still hungry, and they still cried out for land reform and better working conditions. A small group of revolutionaries who called themselves Bolsheviks, or members of the majority, began organizing to seize power. Promising "peace, land, and bread," they attracted many followers, especially in the military. The Russian Army, which had suffered more than 5.5 million casualties in the war, was reluctant to continue fighting. It was eager to follow anyone who could bring peace.

The Bolsheviks were led by Vladimir Ilych Lenin, a man who dreamed of carrying out a communist revolution and establishing a classless society in Russia. Lenin was influenced by the ideas of Karl Marx, a nineteenth-century German economist. According to Marx, capitalism was doomed to fail and be replaced by a classless society

Lenin led the Bolsheviks to a communist revolution in Russia.

known as communism. Workers would eventually rise up against the wealthy business owners.

Marx had predicted that communist revolutions would occur first in the most advanced industrial nations, such as Germany, and much later in nations with more backward economies, such as Russia. But Lenin's message appealed to many Russians. On November 7, 1917, the Bolsheviks stormed the Winter Palace in St. Petersburg, took over the offices of the government, and arrested the officials of Kerensky's government.

True to his word, Lenin gave control of factories to the workers and ordered that farmland be distributed to the peasants. He then signed a peace treaty with Germany in March 1918 to focus his attention on building his new communist nation. The treaty gave up control of some territories that had once been part of the Russian Empire, including Finland, Latvia, Lithuania, Poland, and Ukraine.

Wilson's Fourteen Points

By 1918, the Allies were slowly winning the war. Germany was losing, but far from beaten. Millions of soldiers were already dead or wounded. Many more would surely die in the battles that lay ahead. The world was tired of this brutal war. People in Europe and America wanted it to end. As the fighting continued, President Wilson stepped forward with a plan for peace.

Wilson's plan was called the Fourteen Points. It contained fourteen key ideas for peace. In a speech before Congress on January 8, 1918, Wilson emphasized the need for nations to work together for peace. He did not like what had happened in Europe before the war. Nations had built huge armies and huge empires. They had engaged in secret talks. They had threatened each other. The president felt that these acts had led to war.

Woodrow Wilson: President and Scholar

Thomas Woodrow Wilson was born into a minister's family in 1856. He knew the value of hard work and study. Young Wilson attended Princeton University and two other schools. He then embarked on a career of teaching and writing.

Wilson later returned to Princeton as a professor and went on to become the school's president. In 1910, he was elected governor of New Jersey. Voters liked his honesty and dedication to progressivism and reform. Two years later, in 1912, Woodrow Wilson was elected the twenty-eighth president of the United States. During the 1912 election, Theodore Roosevelt split the Republican vote with William Taft, which allowed the Democratic candidate, Wilson, to win.

Wilson was reelected in 1916 in part because he had kept America out of World War I. However, in April 1917, the president would lead America into the conflict that he hoped would prevent future wars. For his role in ending World War I, Wilson received the 1919 Nobel Peace Prize. Woodrow Wilson died in 1924.

President Wilson presents to Congress the armistice terms that end World War I.

Wilson wanted freedom and cooperation. He proposed that the seas of the world should be open to all nations, that each country should agree to limit the size of its army and navy, and that they should trade with each other fairly and honorably. Most importantly, Wilson thought that countries should discuss matters openly. For this purpose, he suggested an international organization of countries.

Wilson's proposed League of Nations would be a place where diplomats from member nations could meet. They would talk about the world's problems and try to find peaceful solutions. In this way, President Wilson felt that future wars could be avoided. Wilson would have to wait until the war ended, however, to see whether both sides would accept these Fourteen Points.

An End to the Fighting

With the withdrawal of Russian soldiers, Germany now had more troops to throw into battle. Still, the Germans were no match for the Allies, who had been reinforced by more than two million American troops.

In July 1918, at the Second Battle of the Marne, the Allied forces, led by four hundred fifty tanks, smashed through German lines and advanced toward Germany.

By now, the German people were fed up with the war. On October 29, 1918, German sailors at Kiel, Germany, mutinied and called for the establishment of a German republic. On November 9, 1918, Germany's leader Kaiser Wilhelm II, fearing revolution, stepped down and fled to Holland. He was joined two days later by Emperor Charles I, the ruler of Austria-Hungary. On November 11, Germany and the Allies signed an armistice, or peace agreement, and World War I finally came to an end.

The Treaty of Versailles

With the truce in place, leaders of the Allies gathered at Versailles, a palace near the French capital, Paris. They discussed the terms under which they would accept Germany's surrender. President Wilson had earlier proposed Fourteen Points for achieving a just and lasting peace. Great Britain and France, however, disagreed with most of Wilson's ideas. They insisted that Germany receive a harsh punishment. They wanted to break up the Austro-Hungarian and Ottoman empires completely, limit the size of the German military, and force Germany to give up its overseas colonies. They also wanted Germany to pay for the war.

When the German delegates arrived in Versailles, they were shocked. The treaty before them was nothing like the Fourteen Points. It would place a heavy burden on their nation. The Germans protested the treaty as unfair. However, unable to fight any longer, they had to accept the terms of the treaty. The Treaty of Versailles was signed on June 28, 1919. The Great War was officially over.

The Treaty of Versailles angered the German people. They did not believe that their nation had really lost the war. The Germans also refused to accept blame for starting the war. The debt Germany owed to the Allies totaled tens of billions of dollars. It was paid in German ships, trains, money, and natural resources. For years, these debt payments took resources away from German businesses and government. Factories and other businesses closed, and many people lost their jobs. The nation's economy was crippled. The misery and bitterness of the post-war period would help Adolf Hitler and his Nazi Party take control of Germany during the 1930s.

The signing of the Treaty of Versailles signified the end of the Great War.

Congress Rejects the League of Nations

World War I, billed as the war to end wars, had cost the lives of more than ten million soldiers, more than one hundred thousand of them American. To prevent such a catastrophe from occurring in the future, President Wilson proposed the creation of a League of Nations to bring countries together to settle disputes diplomatically.

Wilson had argued tirelessly for the league while in Europe. However, upon returning to the United States, he learned that his own nation was against the idea. Many Americans were unhappy about the war and still did not understand why US soldiers had fought and died so that the countries of Europe could broaden their empires. Americans thought that if they joined the League of Nations, one day the United States might be forced to fight another European war.

Wilson traveled the country to try to convince Americans that membership in the league could help prevent another war. In September 1919, he suffered a stroke that kept him from stirring up public support. Two months later, the US Senate rejected membership to the League of Nations.

Other countries did join the League of Nations, but ultimately it was a failure. However, the League of Nations proved to be a small step toward world peace. It would help inspire the creation of the far more successful United Nations in 1945.

Russian Civil War

Meanwhile in Russia, as Lenin and the Bolsheviks moved the capital from St. Petersburg to Moscow, pockets of resistance to the communists arose in various parts of the huge country. A civil war, which would last three years, broke out between the Reds, or communists, and the Whites, or supporters of the Tsar.

On July 16, 1918, Tsar Nicholas II and his entire family, who were being kept under house arrest in Ekaterinburg, were executed by

Bolsheviks who feared that the White Army might free them and use them as a symbol to rally the Russian people against the new communist government.

Alarmed by developments in Russia and fearing that communism might spread to other countries, the United States and its allies sent thousands of troops to Russia to help the White Army. But by the time the civil war ended in 1920, the communists were in control of Russia.

On December 28, 1922, the communist government in Russia would announce that it was joining with some lands that had one been part of the Russian Empire to create the Union of Soviet Socialist Republics, or Soviet Union. The Soviet Union would eventually conquer and absorb its neighbors in central Asia and eastern Europe.

As the country shifted to a communist way of life, life became better for some Russians. But Russians did not have the freedom and equality they had been promised. By switching to communism, the Russian people had merely traded one harsh rule for another.

Advances in Science, Technology, and Medicine

The 1910s were known for several important scientific and technological advancements. Some were developed because of the war rather than in spite of it. Winning the war depended on superior technology, such as machine guns, tanks, and poison gases. While technology contributed to the Allied victory in World War I, it would play an even greater role in future wars.

Einstein's Theory of Relativity

In 1905, a twenty-six-year-old clerk in the Swiss Patent Office by the name of Albert Einstein had published an article in a German physics journal. It outlined a new way of understanding the universe. In his special theory of relativity, Einstein challenged the accepted notion that space and time are absolute. According to Einstein, motion, space, and time are not absolute but relative to the frame of reference of the observer who is measuring them. At the time, very few people were receptive to Einstein's ideas. Indeed, few could even understand what he was talking about. However, Einstein continued to develop his ideas.

Acceptance of Albert Einstein's brilliant theories would take time.

The Incan city Machu Picchu was rediscovered in 1911.

In 1916, Einstein published his general theory of relativity. He claimed that space is curved by the gravitational forces of bodies in space. Einstein predicted that this could be seen during an upcoming eclipse. On May 29, 1919, British astronomer Arthur Eddington was observing the total eclipse of the sun. He noticed that the light from certain stars was curved as it passed near the sun before reaching the earth. This observation proved Einstein's theory, which would have enormous effects on science and technology in the twentieth century.

Machu Picchu Is Discovered

At an elevation of 7,710 feet, the city of Machu Picchu sits between two sharp peaks in the Andes Mountains of Peru. The five-mile-square fortress city was believed to have been built by the Inca, an American Indian group, around the year AD 400. In 1532, Spanish conquerors arrived in South America and destroyed the Incan civilization. Because Machu Picchu was located in such an inaccessible location, however, the Spaniards never found it. For the next few centuries, Machu Picchu was forgotten. Then in July 1911, an American archaeologist named Hiram Bingham rediscovered Machu Picchu.

Machu Picchu's true purpose is shrouded in mystery. Its houses, temples, and palaces are built of huge stones that fit together perfectly. There are thousands of steps consisting of stone blocks, as well as footholds carved into the rock. Walkways connect plazas, residential areas, terraces, the cemetery, and the major buildings. There is also a huge stone sundial. The Inca are known to have worshiped a sun god, and some archaeologists believe Machu Picchu may have been a religious ceremonial center. Others believe it was a fortress or a palace complex for the royal family.

Trekking to the South Pole

By 1911, most of the faraway corners of the earth had been explored and mapped. The polar regions, however, still offered bold explorers an opportunity to venture into uncharted territory. During the previous decade, American explorer Commander Robert Peary had reached the North Pole on April 6, 1909. The South Pole, however, still awaited discovery. It offered fame and fortune to the first person to tread on it. In the fall of 1911, two polar expeditions, one from Norway and the other from Great Britain, had set up base camps in Antarctica and planned to be the first to reach the South Pole.

A Norwegian explorer named Roald Amundsen and four companions set out for the South Pole on October 19, 1911. They traveled on skis and used sled dogs to carry their supplies. Amundsen's group had an advantage over the British group—their base camp at the Bay of Whales was sixty miles closer to the pole. Just thirteen days later, on November 1, English explorer Robert Falcon Scott set out for the pole from Cape Evans. Scott and his eleven men used Siberian ponies and motorized sledges, as well as dog teams. Scott's expedition, however, was plagued with problems almost from the start. Although November was mid-spring in the Antarctic, the weather was harsh, as was the terrain. Before they were halfway to their destination, the ponies had to be shot, the motors had broken down, and the dog teams had to be sent back, as did seven of the men. These men had been a support group. They were never supposed to be part of the entire journey. Scott and four others continued on to the pole and arrived there on January 18, 1912. But their joy turned to bitter disappointment when they learned that Amundsen had reached the pole a month ahead of them on December 14, 1911.

By this time, Amundsen and his group were well on their way back to their base camp, and they returned there safely on January 25. Luck had now run out for Scott and his companions. They died on the Ross

Roald Amundsen's expedition was the first to reach the South Pole.

British tanks frightened German soldiers during World War I.

Ice Shelf when they were caught in a severe blizzard just eleven miles from their base camp.

Wegener's Theory of Continental Drift

In 1915, German geologist and meteorologist Alfred Wegener published *The Origin of Continents and Oceans*. In it, he proposed a theory of continental drift. Wegener argued that the continents had at one time been joined together in a single mass, which he called Pangaea, that somehow broke up and then drifted apart. He noticed that the west coast of Africa looked as if it fit neatly into the east coast of South America. He also discovered that matching layers of rock and fossil evidence could be found on both sides of the Atlantic Ocean. But Wegener had no idea how the continents could have moved. It was not until the 1960s that geologists would begin to understand the process of plate tectonics.

Technological Advances Win the War

During the Battle of the Somme in France in September 1916, German soldiers were seen running in panic across the fields. They were fleeing from the menacing iron monsters rolling toward them. Because they had never seen tanks before, the Germans' fear was understandable. This was the first time tanks had made their appearance on the battlefield. Developed by British engineers with the support of then-naval commander Winston Churchill, tanks were first produced in England in 1915.

Many other technological innovations were also introduced during the war. Both sides were constantly looking for more deadly methods of killing. In Nashville, Tennessee, the largest explosives factory in the world produced more than one hundred thousand pounds of explosive powder each day. Incendiary bombs and flamethrowers were invented and hastily put into production. The Germans began using poison gas in April 1915, and the Allies soon did the same. Airplanes were loaded with bombs and fitted with machine guns for aerial combat. Germany used zeppelins—huge airships—to attack targets on the ground in Great Britain and France. And beneath the sea, German submarines proved their effectiveness by sinking 6,604 Allied ships.

Leaps in Communication

Alexander Graham Bell had made the first call from one room to another on his newly invented telephone back in 1876. On January 25, 1915, Bell made the first coast-to-coast phone call from San Francisco to New York. Meanwhile, wireless technology had also been rapidly advancing. The telegraph, a form of wireless communication, was invented by Guglielmo Marconi in 1894. In 1912, telegraph operators on the *Titanic* sent wireless distress messages in Morse code as the ship was sinking. Ten nearby ships were alerted and helped rescue the survivors.

Within the next few years, it became possible to transmit voice by a form of wireless communication known as radio. In 1915, the American Telephone and Telegraph Company (AT&T) sent a radio signal across the Atlantic Ocean from the naval station at Arlington, Virginia. In 1916, David Sarnoff, the founder of RCA, proposed to develop radio to bring music into the home through a device called the Radio Music Box. That same year, the experimental radio station 8XK began broadcasting in Pittsburgh. It was soon shut down for the duration of World War I and reopened in 1919. The station received the first Department of Commerce commercial radio license in 1920 and began broadcasting that year as station KDKA in Pittsburgh, Pennsylvania.

Wireless technology furthered global communication.

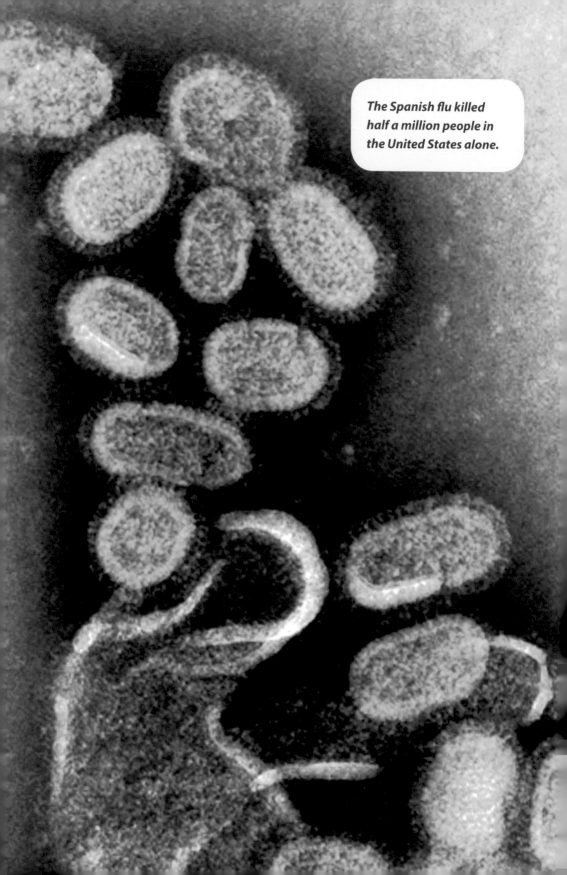

The Spanish flu killed half a million people in the United States alone.

Deadly Flu Kills Millions

People compared it to the Black Death—the bubonic plague that had decimated the population of Europe during the mid-fourteenth century. It was called the Spanish flu because news of the mysterious disease that was killing people throughout Spain first came from Madrid in May 1918. The flu had actually appeared first in China. It spread with amazing speed throughout Asia, Europe, and America, due in great part to World War I.

The highly contagious form of influenza spared neither young nor old, neither civilians nor soldiers. People were afraid to go to school or work. They stayed indoors so they would not get sick. There was no known cure for the Spanish flu, which often developed into pneumonia. Death usually occurred within forty-eight hours of the onset of the first symptoms. In the United States, the Spanish flu virus eventually killed more than half a million people. However, the Spanish flu vanished in 1919 almost as quickly as it came.

Conclusion

The 1910s were a time of enormous change in American life. The wave of immigration to the United States that had been going on for the previous two decades reached a high point. Millions of new arrivals, as well as native-born Americans, were eager to take advantage of the economic opportunities the nation's booming industries offered them. New technologies led to more efficient methods of production. Workers turned to labor unions to fight for better treatment from employers, and they were often the victims of violent attacks when they participated in strikes. Progressives fought for shorter hours, better wages, and safer conditions for workers. They also tried to enact laws prohibiting child labor.

In 1917, President Wilson, who for three years had kept America out of war, decided to lead America into World War I. Also that year, the Bolshevik Revolution took place in Russia, and Vladimir Lenin became the leader of the world's first communist nation. The 1910s in America ended amid massive labor strife and the hysteria of the Red Scare. Many Americans began to yearn for a return to normalcy, which paved the way for the conservative Republican administrations of the 1920s.

Americans during this decade did find ways to have fun by listening to new forms of music, enjoying the novelty of Hollywood movies, and partaking in America's pastime—baseball. But the decade of 1910 to 1919 was also filled with tragedy and sorrow. By 1920, those who had survived tragedies, such as World War I and the influenza epidemic, were ready to have some fun. A new era known as the Roaring Twenties soon began in the United States.

The 1920s were a time of many social changes in America. Women gained the right to vote in national elections. Young women, who became known as flappers, began to wear bold clothing in public. Immigrants and African Americans also sought greater rights as American citizens. During the 1920s, it was illegal to manufacture, sell, or transport alcoholic beverages. This period became known as the Prohibition. Laws banning alcohol had been passed to reduce crime, but they had the opposite effect. Americans continued to drink alcohol during the Prohibition, and gangsters became wealthy by smuggling and selling illegal liquor.

The decade was also known for consumer spending. Factories turned out many new products, such as washing machines and radios. People borrowed money to purchase these products. They also invested their savings in the stock market. The wild spending hid problems in the American economy. The decade closed with a terrible stock market collapse in October 1929. The world soon found itself mired in the Great Depression.

Timeline

1910   The United States is the richest country in the world. The wave of immigration is at its height. The hobble skirt is introduced. Jack Johnson defeats former boxing heavyweight champion James J. Jeffries. Revolution erupts in Mexico. The National Urban League is founded.

1911   In March, a fire at the Triangle Shirtwaist Factory kills more than one hundred women workers. The first Indy 500 is held on Memorial Day. Mexican President Porfirio Díaz resigns from office in May. American archaeologist Hiram Bingham discovers the lost Incan city of Machu Picchu. Norwegian explorer Roald Amundsen arrives at the South Pole in December.

1912   English explorer Robert Scott arrives at the South Pole in January. The Children's Bureau, designed to oppose child labor, is established under the leadership of Julia Lathrop. A strike occurs at textile mills in Lawrence, Massachusetts, which is one of many labor actions that take place during the 1910s. In April, the Titanic sinks. Juliette "Daisy" Low starts her Girl

Scout organization. American Indian athlete Jim Thorpe excels in the Summer Olympics. Theodore Roosevelt makes an unsuccessful run for the presidency on the Progressive party ticket. Roosevelt survives an assassination attempt during his campaign. Democrat Woodrow Wilson is elected president.

1913   In September, UMW miners in Ludlow, Colorado, go on strike against their employer, John D. Rockefeller. Henry Ford creates an assembly line in his automobile plant. The first drive-in gas station opens. The Armory Show in New York introduces new artistic styles, including Cubism. IOC takes away Jim Thorpe's medals and denies his amateur status. General Victoriano Huerta leads a military coup in Mexico.

1914   World War I begins after Archduke Franz Ferdinand is assassinated. In April, the Ludlow mine strike is forcefully ended, which kills many people. Revolutionaries overthrow Huerta in Mexico, and Venustiano Carranza takes over the government. The Panama Canal opens for shipping.

1915   The KKK becomes active when it receives a charter in Georgia. Striking workers are killed by guards during a labor action in Bayonne, New Jersey. In April, boxer Jack Johnson is defeated by Jess Willard. In May, the *Lusitania* is sunk by a German submarine. Girl Scouts of America is incorporated. *Birth of a Nation* is released.

1916 The Keating-Owen Child Labor Act passes. *Intolerance* is released. President Woodrow Wilson sends United States troops to attack Mexican troops under Pancho Villa in response to attacks on American citizens. Albert Einstein publishes his general theory of relativity. The Battle of the Somme takes place in France in September.

1917 President Wilson urges Congress to declare war on Germany. The United States enters World War I. The Bolshevik Revolution begins in Russia. The Immigration Act restricts immigration, especially for Asians. African Americans march in New York to protest lynchings. Race riots take place in Houston and East Saint Louis. In April, Jeanette Rankin takes her seat as the first woman elected to Congress. Original Dixieland Jass Band makes the first jazz recording. Dadaists exhibit their work in New York.

1918 Lenin withdraws Russian troops from World War I in March after signing a peace treaty with Germany. On July 16, Tsar Nicholas II and his family are executed in Russia. The Second Battle of the Marne takes place. On November 9, German Kaiser Wilhelm II steps down from the throne. On November 11, the Allies and Germany sign a peace agreement that ends World War I.

1919 Twenty-five major race riots occur throughout the United States with the worst happening in Chicago. In November, the Palmer-Hoover anticommunist raids begin. The Eighteenth and Nineteenth Amendments to the Constitution are passed. Sir Barton wins the Triple Crown of horse racing. Emiliano Zapata is killed by soldiers under the leadership of Carranza in Mexico. In May, British scientist Arthur Eddington proves the accuracy of Albert Einstein's theory of relativity.

Glossary

ace—A pilot who has shot down five enemy planes.

alliance—A collection of nations or groups working toward a common goal.

armistice—An agreement to stop fighting.

colony—A territory owned or controlled by a distant country.

dogfighting—In war, combat between airplanes.

empire—A powerful nation that controls a great deal of territory.

epicenter—Central point or point where something starts.

genre—Category of art.

Great Migration—Movement of African Americans from the rural South to the urban North and Midwest.

hobble skirt— Long skirt tied near the hem by a straight band, which causes its wearer to hobble.

improvisation—An unplanned change, invention, or creation.

indict—To formally accuse of a crime.

influenza—A viral disease that causes fever, chills, and breathing problems, also know as the flu.

manslaughter—The killing of a person without premeditation.

piecework—Work paid by the amount or number produced.

plugger—Singers who performed requests at music stores.

progressive—Group or ideology calling for social reform or the implementation of liberal changes.

sweatshop—Workshop or factory with poor working conditions and pay.

tsar—Russian emperor.

Further Reading

Books

Grant, R.G. *World War I*. New York: DK Publishing, 2014.

Ingalls, David S. *Hero of the Angry Sky*. Athens, Ohio: Ohio University Press, 2013.

Opdyke, Sandra. *The Flu Epidemic of 1918*. New York: Routledge, 2014.

Remarque, Erich Maria. *All Quiet on the Western Front*. Boston: Little, Brown and Company, 1929.

Richards, Marlee. *America in the 1910s*. Minneapolis, Minn. Twenty First Century, 2009.

Wilson, Andrew. *Shadow of the Titanic*. New York: Atria Books, 2012.

Woolf, Virginia. *Mrs. Dalloway*. London: Hogarth Press, 1925.

Web Sites

fordham.edu/halsall/mod/modsbook39.html
Fordham University's Russian Revolution site includes many entries about the Russian Revolution.

memory.loc.gov/ammem/nfhtml
The Library of Congress has archived recordings of political candidates during this decade.

encyclopedia.1914-1918-online.net/home/
The International Encyclopedia of the First World War contains a wealth of information about the Great War.

pbs.org/wgbh/amex/influenza/
This PBS companion site includes facts, personal anecdotes, and other information about the 1918 influenza epidemic.

Movies

Iron-Jawed Angels. Directed by Katja von Garnier. New York: HBO Films, 2004.

A historical drama about the women's suffrage movement.

Titanic. Directed by James Cameron. Century City, Calif.: 20th Century Fox, 1997.

A dramatic love story of two star-crossed lovers onboard the *Titanic.*

Index

R

race relations, 11, 12, 43
ragtime, 31, 34
Rankin, Jeanette, 22, 61
Red Scare, 8, 20, 84
relativity, 72
Rockefeller, John D., 19
Rogers, Will, 36
Roosevelt, Theodore, 48, 50, 51, 65
Russian Revolution. *See* Bolshevik Revolution.

S

Sanger, Margaret, 23
Second Battle of the Marne, 67
Sixteenth Amendment, 48, 51
Society of American Indians, 61
South Pole, 76
Spanish flu, 83, 84
submarines, 7, 26, 58, 61, 80
suffragette suit, 32
Summer Olympics, 43, 45
sweatshops, 15

T

Taft, William Howard, 48, 65
Thorpe, Jim, 45, 46
Tin Pan Alley, 34
Titanic, 7, 23, 24, 80
Treaty of Versailles, 68
Triangle Shirtwaist fire, 15
Triple Alliance, 57
Triple Crown, 46
Triple Entente, 57

U

United Mine Workers of America (UMW), 16, 19
United States Children's Bureau, 16
United States Congress, 16, 22, 51, 61, 70
United States Constitution, 8, 22, 48, 51

V

van Gogh, Vincent, 41
vaudeville, 36
Villa, Francisco "Pancho," 53, 54

W

Wegener, Alfred, 79
Wilhelm II, Kaiser of Germany, 67
Wilson, Woodrow, 8, 19, 26, 51, 54, 58, 61, 64, 65, 67, 68, 70, 84
Wobblies, 16, 19
Women's Christian Temperance Union (WCTU), 20, 23
Woolf, Virginia, 40
World War I, 7, 11, 20, 26, 58, 59, 61, 62, 64, 65, 67, 68, 72, 80, 83, 84

Z

Zapata, Emiliano, 53, 54
Ziegfeld Follies, 36
Zimmermann telegram, 61